Dear O.B.D,

This is a gratitude to life, a tribute to the divine that guides our steps. I thank God for all the blessings and, above all, for placing you in my path. I believe that the true purpose of existence is to give meaning to the lives around us, and you, dear O.B.D, are the deepest meaning of my journey.

Your love fills every empty space, brightens every shadow, and adds color to every moment. You are the reason why my life has such a special purpose.

Loving you is a divine gift, and for that, I express my gratitude to God for placing you at the center of my heart.

With all my love,

David Lucas

2024

This Book Belongs to:

D.L.G.D. ©
DLGD publications

Test Color Page

www.ingramcontent.com/pod-product-compliance
Lightning Source LLC
Chambersburg PA
CBHW080729260726
48660CB00010B/3759
9798878978989